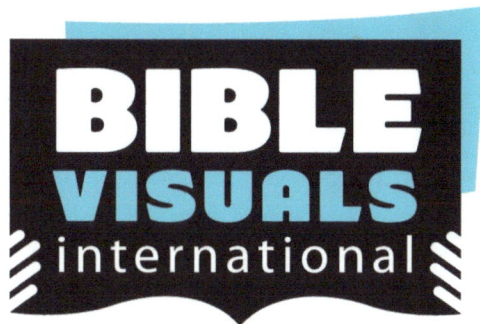

Helping Children See Jesus

ISBN: 978-1-933206-83-7

A Chosen Friend
A Story of Mexico

Authors: Karen Puckett, Karen E. Weitzel
Illustrator: Barb Alber
Typesetting and Layout: Morgan Melton, Patricia Pope

© 2018 Bible Visuals International
PO Box 153, Akron, PA 17501-0153
Phone: (717) 859-1131
www.biblevisuals.org

RELATED ITEMS

To access related items (such as activities, memory verse posters and translated texts) please visit our web store at shop.biblevisuals.org and enter 5090 in the search box on the page.

FREE TEXT DOWNLOAD

To access a FREE printable copy of the teaching text (PDF format) in English or other available languages, enter S5090DL in the search box. Add the item to your cart, and use coupon code XTACSV17 at checkout. Once your order is processed you will receive an email with a link to the free download.

- 1 -

For God so loved the world, that He gave His only begotten Son, that whosoever believeth in Him should not perish, but have everlasting life. John 3:16

Christ died for our sins according to the Scriptures . . . was buried, and . . . rose again the third day according to the Scriptures.

1 Corinthians 15:3b, 4

I will never leave thee, nor forsake thee. Hebrews 13:5b

Continue . . . in the things which thou hast learned . . . That from a child thou hast known the holy scriptures which are able to make thee wise unto salvation through faith . . . in Christ Jesus.

2 Timothy 3:14a, 15

Ye have not chosen Me, but I have chosen you, and ordained you, that ye should go and bring forth fruit, and that your fruit should remain.

John 15:16a

A man that hath friends must shew himself friendly: and there is a friend that sticketh closer than a brother.

Proverbs 18:24

NOTE TO THE TEACHER

This five-chapter missionary story is based on true accounts of mission work in Mexico. Indian culture, superstition, opposition to and receipt of the Gospel are seen through the eyes of Rosa, an Aztec Indian. Location, tribe, language and some cultural differences may be changed so that the story can represent other Indian villages and mission work in some Central and South American countries.

PRONUNCIATION GUIDE

Tortilla: tor-tee´-yuh

¿Cómo está usted?: Koh´-moh ays-tah oos-tayd´ (How are you?)

Muy bien, gracias: Mwee byayn´ grah-syas (Very well, thank you)

Buenas noches: Bway´-nohz noch-as (Good night)

Señora: se-nyoh´-rä

Petate: pe-tä´-te

Hermana: er-mä´-nä

Hermano: er-mä´-noh

Machete: muh-shet´-e

GLOSSARY

Petate: sleeping mat made of palm used by natives in Central and South America.

Tortilla: a pancake, made of Indian corn mashed and baked on an earthen pan.

Señora: a married lady; same as English "Mrs."

Hermano: brother

Hermana: sister

Machete: cutlass, chopping-knife, cane-knife.

The *aim* of the lesson:

1. To introduce the truth that God loves all people
2. To show how people on the mission field sometimes react to and oppose the Gospel

The verse to be memorized:

For God so loved the world, that He gave His only begotten Son, that whosoever believeth in Him, should not perish, but have everlasting life. (John 3:16)

Rosa trudged along the narrow dirt path under the orange and tangerine trees. The hardened mud felt cool to her feet. She was tired from gathering sticks for the cooking fire. The bundle on her back poked her shoulders with every step.

"María got the easy job today," she grumbled, adjusting the headband that held the burlap around the sticks. "She gets to sit and rub the corn off the cobs. I like to make the corn kernels plop in the basket, too, but María says six-year-olds can't shell corn as fast as ten-year-olds."

Show Illustration #1

Spying an orange along the path, Rosa stooped over and picked up the bright fruit. Her brown fingers quickly peeled the bumpy skin. She licked the sticky, sweet juice from her hands as she ate. A rustle in the bushes near their hut made Rosa look up.

"Rosa! Rosa, where are you?" a girl's voice called softly. Rosa wiped her hands over her faded red dress. She tugged again at the headband holding the sack of sticks on her back.

"I'm coming, María," Rosa shouted, heading for the village.

A thin girl ran down the path, her shiny black braid swinging behind her back. "Sh! Don't talk loudly, Rosa. Follow me. I want you to hear what our neighbors are telling Mama. Leave the sticks here, behind this bush. We can get them later for the cooking fire."

"What's happened?" Rosa asked and grabbed the skirt of María's dress.

"Nothing–yet, but you'll hear. It's about the missionaries," María whispered as they tiptoed to the back of their hut. Standing in the shade of the thatched roof, they peered through the tiny cracks in the wall of sticks.

Show Illustration #2

Rosa could see Mama at the far end of the hut. She was bending over the stove made of dried mud and rocks. Rosa watched Mama lift a pot off the fire and pour coffee for the guests. One large lady waved her hands and talked loudly.

"Those people are foreigners. They should go back to their country."

"Yes!" agreed another neighbor leaning forward. "Why did they come here? Maybe they'll steal our children."

Rosa wound her fingers around the sticks in the wall of the hut. *Oh, I hope they won't steal me,* she thought then trembled, imagining how horrid and lonely it would be not to live with her family.

"I think they are sons of the devil," a third Indian lady continued.

Mama interrupted. "No, no! These missionaries are our friends. They haven't come to harm us. They only want to help us. They believe in God and want to teach us what the Bible says."

"Ha!" exclaimed the fat lady. "How can that help us?"

"The Bible says that God loves us," Rosa's mother said. "God loved us so much that He sent Jesus to make a way for us to be forgiven of our sin."

"Stop, stop!" the heavy lady cried in alarm. "We don't want these foreigners teaching us that."

María touched Rosa's shoulder. "Let's go get the wood now. Mama will need it for cooking dinner."

As the girls headed for the path, María whispered, "I know Mama and Papa like the missionaries. They've known them for a long time. But it makes me sad that some of our neighbors think the missionaries are bad."

"It makes me afraid," Rosa confided to her older sister. "Sometimes when I go through the village, people tell me that Mama and Papa should not be friends with the foreigners. They say if I am nice to the missionaries, they won't let their children be my friends. I'm afraid I'll never have a friend."

The next morning Rosa awakened early when she heard the rooster crowing outside. A loud crackle at the other end of the hut meant Mama had started the fire in the mud stove. Kicking off her blanket, she sat up on her petate. The palm mat felt warm where she had lain. She rubbed her eyes, then tried to smooth the wrinkles out of her dress.

"María. Rosa. It's wash day," Mama called. "Fold your blankets and roll your mats. I have sweet coffee and bread for you. We'll take breakfast to Papa later."

Rosa reached over and tickled María before jumping up. Laughing at her sister, she picked up the hairbrush and quickly pulled it through her long hair. She was hungry and the coffee smelled so good that she couldn't wait to eat.

"We must always thank God for our food, Rosa," Mama admonished as Rosa reached for the bread. The little girl dipped a piece of bread in the coffee, then popped it in her mouth. Mama continued, "We'll eat breakfast with Papa later in the cornfield, but before then I need water for washing."

After the early morning meal, Rosa grabbed her small bucket and followed María to the creek. Kneeling on a rock, Rosa said, "We'll use the buckets I carry for drinking and cooking water."

"And we'll use mine for washing dishes," María answered, lifting her bucket onto her head. "Then we'll both carry water for washing clothes. Mama needs lots. If it were rainy season she could wash at the creek."

Show Illustration #3

Mama balanced the long, wooden washtub on the plank table outdoors. Rosa and María poured in the water. Slosh-slap-splash. Slosh-splash. Mama scrubbed the clothes one at a time, then María spread them over bushes to dry in the sun.

A fat, mud-caked pig ambled around the side of the hut snorting and sniffing in the dust. Mama turned just as the pig moved towards a bush where María had placed a dress. "María!" she cried in alarm. "The clothes!"

María pulled a stick from the wood pile and running to the pig, thumped it across its back. "Go! Go away!" The pig grunted and wandered into the woods.

Show Illustration #4

As the bright, hot sun dried the clothes, Mama ground corn on a large stone slab. Back and forth she rolled a tube-shaped stone over the kernels. Then with quick even pats, she formed tortillas and put them on a big, thin, round clay dish. While the tortillas baked, Mama prepared the big breakfast of black beans, scrambled eggs cooked with chile and onion, and coffee. Rosa packed some of the food in a large bowl. "Papa will like your breakfast, Mama," she said shyly.

Mama led the girls through the village to reach the cornfield where Papa was working. "Look," cried María pointing ahead. Rosa saw the missionaries coming along the trail through the trees. Before the missionaries saw them, Mama turned onto a side path that led to the cornfield. Rosa ran ahead and stepped behind a tree. She peeked out and looked down the trail, but the

missionaries continued through the village. She was safe, but decided to stay close to Mama all day.

The next morning on the way home from church, Rosa and María gathered sticks. Returning to the hut, Rosa caught her breath. "María," she whispered, "the missionaries are here." She stared at the open doorway. Her heart beat wildly.

A man and woman sat at the small table drinking coffee and eating bread with Papa. *Mama even has an embroidered cloth on the table,* Rosa noticed. She edged closer to the door to listen.

"Rosa is just the right age. We're sure that you'll be glad if you send her. She'll learn to read and write, and we'll teach her about Jesus," said the man.

"But she's only six years old," said Papa. "That is too young to leave home."

"Yes, but you'll be able to visit her on weekends," responded the woman. "The school year will pass quickly. Before you know it, summer will come."

"I don't know what to decide," said Papa slowly, looking over at Mama.

Rosa turned and fled into the woods. She crouched behind a bush and peered through the branches, watching María slip into the hut. "No, no, no," she sobbed. "Why can't María go instead of me?"

After the missionaries left, Rosa ran back to the hut. Papa stood in front of the door and appeared to be puzzled. "What did they want?" she cried. "Why were they talking about me? Are they going to steal me?"

"No, Rosa, don't be afraid," soothed Papa, hugging her. "Run and bring Grandmother so I can explain everything to the family. She won't like what the missionaries suggested, but she is the oldest member of the family and should be here."

Show Illustration #5

When Rosa returned with Grandmother, everyone sat around the table.

Slowly Papa began, "The missionaries want Rosa to go to school. She would live in town where they have a home for village children and orphans."

Grandmother interrupted, "Would they teach her about their Jesus?"

"Yes," said Papa firmly.

"It would be wonderful for Rosa to learn to read and write. And there are no schools here in our village," Mama said quickly. "But it would be hard to have her live away from home for so long."

Grandmother sputtered some words no one understood. She leaned forward. Her dark eyes glared at Papa. "If you let her go, you will never see her again! Never! Those evil people will kidnap and sell her."

Her sharp voice sent needles of fear through Rosa. "Will they kidnap me, Papa? Will they?" she cried.

Mama pulled Rosa to her. "Rosa, Rosa. No, they won't kidnap you. We love you and would never let anything like that happen. The missionaries are our friends. They wouldn't lie to us."

Sitting close to Mama, Rosa felt safe. She knew Mama and Papa would not do anything to hurt her.

Grandmother pounded the table with her hand. "All the neighbors will say you don't love Rosa anymore. They'll be right! You want to get her out of the house so you don't have to feed her and spend money to care for her. Well, she can come and live with me! She is my favorite granddaughter. Come along, Rosa. Let's go now!"

Grandmother rose quickly and grabbed Rosa's wrist. Rosa pulled away and leaned against her mother.

"Wait!" said Papa sternly. "We do not want to get rid of Rosa. The missionaries asked if we would allow her to go to school. I will make the decision either to keep Rosa in the village or take her to town. Before I do, I need to pray and think about this more. No one is taking Rosa anywhere until I know what God wants us to do."

As the days passed, Rosa went to Grandmother's only when sent on an errand. One day a neighbor stopped her. "Your parents don't really love you. If they did, they would not let you leave the village. They are going to sell you. You'll never see. . ."

Rosa shouted, "That's not true! Mama and Papa do love me. They won't sell me." She ran past the startled woman to Grandmother's house. Outside the door, she dropped a bundle of sticks and turned to leave. She loved Grandmother, but her strange ways frightened her more than the things the neighbors were saying. Grandmother was a witch doctor. She listened to the spirit world.

"Rosa, come here," Grandmother called from her dark hut.

Rosa entered slowly. She remembered the times she hid and trembled in the shadowy corner watching Grandmother do scary magic. *I hope she doesn't do any now,* she thought, glancing around the smoky room.

Show Illustration #6

Grandmother hobbled away from the stove. "Rosa, if you go to that school, you must not make friends with the missionaries as your parents have. And, you must never forget all I've taught you about the spirits. Come, sit down," she ordered. She pushed Rosa onto a bench and sat on a chair in front of her.

Rosa clutched the edge of the bench and dug her fingernails into the wood. She wanted to say that Mama needed her at home, but she couldn't talk. What was Grandmother going to do?

Chapter 2

WANTED: ONE FRIEND

The *aim* of the lesson:

1. To explain that Jesus Christ died on the cross, was buried, and rose again to make forgiveness of sin available to everyone
2. To show how mission schools teach national children

The verse to be memorized:

Christ died for our sins according to the Scriptures; and . . . was buried, and . . . rose again the third day according to the Scriptures. (1 Corinthians 15:3b-4)

Show Illustration #6

Grandmother's dark eyes stared hard at Rosa. "Now, when you see a black cat, is it really a cat?"

Rosa stuttered, "I . . . I think so."

"No!" Grandmother shouted. "It's a spirit. And when you see an owl, you will remember the spirits sent it." Turning around, Grandmother waved her arm at the back of the hut. "Don't ever forget how you hid behind those petate and watched me heal people. The spirits came and used me to heal those who were ill."

Rosa shivered as Grandmother walked toward a shelf. "See? I use these candles, herbs, eggs, and whiskey. Sometimes I hold the sick person's clothing in front of the fire–like this." She pulled a piece of cloth from a bench and shook it in front of the stove. "Then, Rosa, I throw my secret powder in the fire. If a vision of a coffin appears, the person will die. If I see a person, the sick will live. What I see always happens, doesn't it?"

Rosa shuddered. "Yes, . . . yes, Grandmother."

"And, Rosa," Grandmother continued, "don't believe anything the missionaries tell you about their Jesus. They will tell you lies. They will not teach you about the spirit world. If you believe what they teach, I'll . . ." she threatened and shook her fist at Rosa.

Abruptly Grandmother turned and threw powder in the fire. Flames flared up and the old woman began her strange chants. Rosa crept out of the hut and ran home.

Show Illustration #8

"Rosa," Mama called from before the mud stove, "the floor needs to be swept."

"Mama," Rosa's voice faltered. "Don't send me to Grandmother's again. She frightens me. Send María next time," the little girl begged.

Mama hugged her daughter. "You won't see Grandmother much more."

"Why not?" asked Rosa in surprise.

"Because Papa and I are taking you to the school in town next week," Mama replied.

Rosa quivered. "The missionaries? Will they steal me?" she stammered.

Mama hugged her more tightly. "No, no, Rosa. The missionaries love children. They will teach you to read and write. Few of the other children in our village can do that. And you'll hear more about Jesus. We can't teach you much about Him . . . ."

Rosa burst into tears. "Grandmother says I shouldn't believe anything about Jesus."

"What Grandmother believes is wrong, Rosa. Jesus is kind and good. Papa and I believe in Him. He has taken away our fear of the spirits and has made us happy."

"Mama," Rosa interrupted looking up through her tears, "will María go to school, too?"

"No, Rosa, only you. María is older and I need her to stay home and help me."

"But . . . but, I'll be all alone!" Rosa cried. "I've never been away from the village . . . or, . . . or you. I won't know anyone at the school. I won't have any friends."

Mama patted her head. "But you will make friends at school. Now, sweep the floor while I prepare dinner." Rosa took the broom handle and swished the long grasses furiously over the mud floor.

The week passed quickly. The day Rosa dreaded finally arrived. She watched Mama pack her few clothes in the straw bag. Then Papa picked it up. Rosa walked out of the village between her parents. As she turned and looked up through the trees, Grandmother and María waved to her.

They walked until sounds from the village were muffled by the tramp of their feet on the path. The sun rose higher in the sky over the gray-green mountains around them. Rosa grew tired and thirsty. A sip of cool water from the gourd Mama carried moistened her parched lips.

After a while, they came to a wide, smooth road. "This will soon lead to town, Rosa," Papa said. Slowly they walked down into the valley.

Suddenly Rosa stopped. The ground was shaking and a loud roaring noise came up the road. Rosa stared. Something big and dark raced towards them. It smelled awful and rattled and roared as it approached. She wanted to scream, but the cry stuck in her throat. Then as quickly as the monster came, it was gone. Swirls of dust whipped Rosa's dress.

"Papa," Rosa whispered.

"That was just a truck, Rosa," said her father. "It's nothing to fear. Always walk on the side of the road and you will be safe. You will see many trucks in town."

As they entered town, Rosa looked from side to side as fast as she could. Smelly trucks and crowded buses wove around bikes and people on the rough cement streets. A crowd of laughing children surrounded an ice cream cart. Horns honked. Babies cried from their mother's backs. Men argued in open doorways. Rosa felt dizzy from all the excitement and leaned against Mama.

"Aren't . . . aren't there any trees here? And . . . and will I live in a place like that?" she asked pointing to a house squeezed in a row of similar queer, square buildings.

Show Illustration #9

Papa laughed. "No, no, people in town live in adobe or cement houses. Up there in the Children's Home is where you will live." He pointed to a hill covered with trees. A long white building with a metal roof was nestled along a curve in the winding road.

As they approached the building, a missionary lady came out of the Home. She greeted them with a smile. "¿Cómo está usted?" she asked.

Rosa wrinkled her forehead. "What is she saying, Mama?"

"I don't know, Rosa. She isn't speaking Aztec. She is speaking Spanish," Mama whispered.

Rosa heard her father talking. She stared at him. "Mama, listen to Papa. He talks like the missionary!"

"Yes. Your father has learned to speak some Spanish because he comes to town so often," Mama replied.

Rosa's father and the missionary spoke together for a while. Then he introduced Rosa to the missionary. She spoke kindly to Rosa, then bowed her head and prayed. Papa said afterwards, "Rosa, Mrs. Peters doesn't speak Aztec very well. She prayed in Spanish and asked God that you would be the first child from our village to accept Jesus."

Rosa looked at the ground. She rubbed her shoe along a crack in one of the flat rocks beneath their feet. *Grandmother doesn't want me to believe that*, she thought. *Mama and Papa do. I wish she had prayed that I would have a friend. That's what I really want.*

Her parents said goodbye and Rosa followed the missionary into the Home.

"Rosa, this is where you will sleep," Mrs. Peters said slowly in Aztec. She unrolled the girl's petate on a lower bunk bed. "Angelica sleeps above you on the top bunk. She will help you learn the rules. But now it's time to eat. Come, I'll take you to the dining room. Oh, I almost forgot. We speak only Spanish in the Home, but you'll learn it quickly."

Rosa followed her to a noisy room full of children.

That night as rain drummed loudly on the metal roof, Rosa curled up on her bunk in the dark and sobbed. "Oh, Mama, Papa," she cried, "come take me home. The rules, they are too hard and the Spanish I don't understand."

Show Illustration #10

The next morning an older girl from town ran up to Rosa and spoke to her in Spanish. Rosa looked at the ground. *I don't know what she's saying*, she thought. *I don't know how to talk to her.*

Several other girls gathered. "Ha, ha," they laughed, pointing at Rosa. "You can't speak Spanish! You can't speak Spanish."

As they continued to chant, Rosa looked up quickly. In Aztec, she shouted, "Stop teasing me!"

The girls burst out laughing again. "You sound so funny."

Rosa turned and ran into the building. *I wish María was here. Or, . . . or that I had a friend who liked me. Angelica doesn't.* She stood trembling beside her small wooden bunk bed remembering the horrid faces Angelica made every time she saw Rosa. *I don't like it here. I want to go home and never come back.* She pulled a piece of palm from the petate on her bunk. *When Mama and Papa come to market on Saturday, I'll go home with them.* Tears trickled down her cheeks onto her uniform making dark spots. She listened to the shouts of the children outdoors. It was quiet in the dormitory, and she felt all alone.

Rosa woke early the next morning. *Only three more days and then it's Saturday.* She kept the secret to herself. Dressing quickly, she straightened her bedding, then glanced across the room. Angelica had stopped sweeping the floor and was trying to rouse Lola who was still asleep. The older girl struggled to wake up. "You'll be late again, Lola," Angelica scolded as she put the broom in the corner.

Rosa gathered her papers and pencil. She touched the point of her pencil. "Ouch!" Yes, it was sharp enough for classes. A bell rang. Another school day had begun. Rosa hurried to the classroom.

Her teacher stood beside the door. "¿Cómo está usted, Rosa?"

"Muy bien, gracias," Rosa answered in Spanish. She felt her cheeks get warm as she looked shyly at the other children. Those close to the door smiled at her. Rosa listened carefully in class. She was surprised at how much she could understand.

That night Rosa couldn't sleep. She lay on her bunk and listened to the rain beat against the roof. *Today was a good day,* she thought. *The missionary looked happy tonight when I said "Buenas noches."*

On Saturday, Rosa waited eagerly outside for her parents. Papa greeted her in Spanish and she answered him. How proud he looked as he listened to the Spanish she spoke hesitantly.

"María misses you," Mama said giving Rosa a piece of candy.

"I miss her, too!" Rosa said, switching to Aztec. "Mama, may I go back with you today? I . . . I want to go home."

"And not go to school?" Mama asked.

"School . . . it's so hard. And, I'm lonely, Mama. I don't have any friends," Rosa cried.

"But you will learn and you will make friends, Rosa," Papa spoke up. "Stay at school a little longer. If it is still too hard for you, then you may come home. We will see you next Saturday on market day, but now we must go. It is a long walk back to the village."

Rosa watched her parents walk down the hill. "They won't take me home," she whispered. "Maybe they don't want me there." Crying, she ran into the building and threw herself onto her bunk. She felt all alone.

Show Illustration #11

As the weeks passed, Rosa became excited about learning. Each day she understood more Spanish. She no longer begged her parents to take her home when they visited on Saturdays.

One day during Bible class, Mrs. Peters opened her Bible and said to the children, "The Lord Jesus taught people about God. He did many miracles and healed many who were sick. But some people did not like what Jesus said and did. They planned to kill him."

Rosa listened. She watched the missionary put on the flannel-board a figure of Christ hanging on the cross.

Mrs. Peters continued, " '. . . Christ died for our sins according to the Scriptures; and was buried, and rose again the third day.' Everyone except the Lord Jesus has sinned (Romans 3:23). God says sin must be punished. The punishment for sin is death (Romans 6:23). Because the Lord Jesus is perfect, He could be punished for sin–your sin, mine, and the sin of everyone. Jesus allowed wicked men to nail Him to a cross where He died."

Rosa wiggled on the bench as she remembered angrily breaking Jose's pencil and stealing candy from Angelica. She, Rosa, had sinned.

The missionary told how kind men buried Jesus in a new tomb. Then on the third day after He died, Jesus came alive.

How can that be? thought Rosa cocking her head in surprise. *Nobody comes back to life after they die. I have seen people buried. They never came alive again.*

Mrs. Peters removed the cross from the flannelboard. "The Bible says many people saw Jesus after He came alive. After spending time with His followers, Jesus returned to Heaven. Someday He is coming back to take to Heaven all who believe in Him." The missionary paused, looking at the class. "Do you believe Jesus died and rose again? That He was punished for your sin?" she asked quietly. "If you do, come talk to me after class. You can pray and ask God to forgive your sin. Then Jesus will become your Saviour. He'll be a friend who is always with you."

Rosa stared at the missionary. *I'd like a friend like that, someone who is always with me.* Then she remembered Grandmother's warning: "The missionaries will tell you lies. Don't believe what they teach."

The Bible class was over, and so was school for the day. Rosa walked past Mrs. Peters to the door. She was sure the teacher could hear her heart beating. *I want to believe in Jesus,* Rosa thought, *but what will Grandmother do to me if I become a Christian? Maybe what the missionaries teach are lies.* But in her heart, Rosa knew the missionaries spoke the truth. A troubled, unhappy little girl walked slowly to the dormitory.

Chapter 3
ROSA FINDS HER FRIEND

The *aim* of the lesson:

1. To teach that when a person receives the Lord Jesus as Savior, he will never be alone
2. To show how sometimes it takes years before a missionary sees a person accept Jesus as Savior

The verse to be memorized:

I will never leave thee, nor forsake thee. (Hebrews 13:5b)

At the end of her fourth year at the Children's Home, Rosa waited impatiently for the graduation ceremony to end. Soon her parents would arrive to take her home for the school break. She watched the older students receive their diplomas. *Maybe I should stay. It would be nice to have a diploma.* Then she remembered how hard it was to study. *No, I will still ask Papa to stay home after this is over, just before we leave for the village.*

After the program, Rosa pushed through the crowd. Her parents were walking towards Mrs. Peters.

Show Illustration #9

"Papa," she called, running to him. "Papa, I want to stay home in the village for good and not come back when school starts again. May I?" she pleaded. "I can read and write now–and speak Spanish. The uniforms cost so much. And Mama needs help with the new baby." She stopped, breathless.

Papa looked at Mama, then Rosa. He nodded his head. "Yes, Rosa, your Mama does need help. María does well caring for your little brothers, but she can't watch baby Felicia, too. You may stay, but we must tell the missionaries."

Mrs. Peters looked at Rosa. "I will miss you," she said. "I know you will be a good helper. Practice your reading and writing so you don't forget what you've learned. Remember what we've taught you about Jesus. I'll pray for you."

Rosa worked hard at home. Within a few days, she was caring for her little sister, Felicia. When the baby cried, Rosa placed her carefully in the wooden box which swung from a rope attached to a ceiling rafter.

"See?" she said to her young brothers. "The baby likes to swing. It makes her fall asleep."

Rosa soon got into the daily routine of gathering wood, washing clothes, helping Mama. But it was caring for Felicia that Rosa enjoyed most. The baby quickly outgrew the wooden box and soon toddled around the hut.

One hot afternoon, Rosa returned from the creek carrying a bucket of water on her head. She watched a well-dressed Mexican woman enter their hut.

I wonder who she is? Rosa thought as she followed the lady inside and put the bucket beside the mud stove.

"I need four girls to work for a rich family in Mexico City," the lady was saying to Mama. "The girls will cook, clean, wash, just as they do now. They will live with the family."

"I don't know," Mama replied. "I need María to help me. Rosa is a hard worker, too, but she is only twelve."

"The family needs the girls for only a few months," said the stranger. "Think of the money Rosa will earn."

"But I don't know these people. What are they like?" persisted Mama.

"Oh, you don't have to worry. They are good people–Christians, even. Your daughter will be happy with them," the lady said. She smiled at Rosa.

Each day the stranger visited the village looking for girls willing to go. Finally four families agreed to send their daughters. Rosa and three older girls, whom she hardly knew, were chosen. They followed the lady down the mountain to the bus stop. The sun was hot and the bus was late. The longer they waited, the more nervous Rosa became.

"I'm scared," whispered Juana. "I've never ridden on a bus."

"I haven't either," Rosa said. Even in the heat, she felt cold. Her teeth chattered. Finally a crowded, noisy bus arrived.

Show Illustration #13

The road curved over the mountains. The bus driver drove fast and the girls felt sick as they were thrown from side to side. As they sped down the last hill, the road straightened and the girls relaxed.

"I wonder what the family will be like," said Juana.

"Oh, they are Christians," exclaimed Rosa. "That means they believe the Bible. They'll be like my parents."

"I didn't know you were a Christian, Rosa," said Flora in surprise.

"I'm not, really. Not like my parents," said Rosa slowly. "But I believe a lot of the Bible." She turned on the seat and stared out the window. Cars–some colorful, others rusty and rattling–whizzed around dirty trucks. *Mama and Papa can't come to this city like they did when I was at the Children's Home.* Suddenly she felt fearful and lonely. The bus lurched and Rosa fell against Juana.

The older girl laughed and hugged Rosa. "I'm glad I don't ride this every day!" she exclaimed.

Rosa straightened her dress and smiled. *I think Juana likes me,* she thought, sliding back onto the seat.

"Look! Look at those big buildings," cried Christina pointing out the window.

"And all those people," Rosa added in amazement.

Cars honked, brakes squealed. When the bus stopped, the girls clung together and followed the lady off the bus to the subway. People shouted and shoved. The underground train swayed back and forth as it sped through eerie tunnels. Rosa was happy when they boarded another bus; even happier when they stopped before the largest house she had ever seen. The long trip was over.

As the girls went up the walk, a tall, well-dressed woman called to them from the center of the entryway. "I am Señora Martinez," she said brusquely. "I have been expecting you. Come along now and follow me. I will show you your room and what you are to do."

Rosa glanced at Juana who stared at the lady. The older girl's mouth dropped open, her dark eyes widened in astonishment.

Show Illustration #14

Rosa trembled. How harsh and stern Señora Martinez treated them. Quickly Rosa stepped behind Juana and followed her through the house listening to the lady. In one room, she passed an altar with a picture hanging above it. Señora Martinez saw her puzzled look. "That is a picture of the virgin Mary, girls. In this house we pray to her."

That night Rosa and the others watched the family burn candles in front of the altar and pray. *Mama and Papa don't have such things. And they don't pray like this,* she observed. *I don't think the Martinez family believes in God the same way my parents do.*

The girls worked hard for four days. The fifth morning Señora Martinez called them together and said, "I can use only one servant, so I will choose the best worker. The rest will work for other families." She looked carefully at each girl. "Rosa, you will stay with me," she stated. "Juana, Flora, Christina, gather your belongings. I will take you to your new homes immediately."

Rosa stared at the floor as the girls left the room. *That lady lied to us,* Rosa thought. *She said all of us would work for one family. Now I'm the only one. I wish Juana could have stayed, too. I'm sure we could have been friends.*

Sra. Martinez turned to Rosa. "Today is a special day. I want you to clean this house until everything shines. When I return I will inspect it thoroughly." She turned to the girls in the hallway. "Come along with me." With a click, she closed the door.

Rosa ran and tried the handle. "Oh, no! I'm locked in!" she cried as she rattled the knob. She leaned against the door. "I'm really alone now," she whispered.

Remembering the Señora's orders, Rosa began working. She washed dishes and did the laundry. She swept the floors and dusted furniture. Hours later, as she folded the clean clothes, Señora Martinez returned. Rosa followed her fearfully through the house. "Very well, Rosa. Put away the clothes now."

Show Illustration #15

Rosa carried the garments to the bedrooms. Passing a window, she saw a man in a long black robe approach the house. A gold cross on a chain hung around his white collar. *Is he the reason why today is special?* Rosa wondered. She heard the door open.

Señora Martinez welcomed the man graciously. "We're so glad you've come to bless our new home," she said sweetly. She led him to each room in the house.

Rosa hurried from room to room to avoid meeting the man. As she passed a doorway, she saw him sprinkle water and heard him utter a prayer. She listened to Señora Martinez speak softly to the visitor. *Why can't she be that kind to me?* Rosa thought as she slipped into another room.

Early one evening several weeks later as Rosa sat in her room, Señora Martinez walked in. "What are you doing, Rosa?" she asked sharply.

"I'm writing a letter to my family," Rosa answered, clutching the paper tightly.

"Let me see it." Señora Martinez pulled the paper from the startled girl. "So, you want to go home? Well, you may not. You haven't worked for me long enough."

"But . . . but," stammered Rosa. "The lady who brought me here said I would work in the city for a few months. I have been here six months and now I want to go home."

"That may be," Señora Martinez replied, "but matters have changed. You are staying longer even though your family has written asking you to come home." The Señora strode toward the door.

"My letter, Señora," Rosa pleaded. "Please may I have my letter?"

Señora Martinez stopped at the door and faced the girl. "No! You may not have it. And, you are never to mail another letter to your family. I shall send them a photograph of you so they will know you are well." She started through the doorway, then paused and spoke rapidly. "In the letter I received, your father said your older sister died. Good night." The door slammed shut behind her.

Rosa stared in shock at the closed door. "Oh, Mama, Papa. How I wish I were at home. María, . . . oh, María!" Rosa threw herself onto the bed and sobbed.

The night had darkened to a deep blue-black sky before Rosa's sobs subsided. She rolled over and rubbed her eyes with the back of her hand. Reaching for the light beside her bed, she bumped the Bible she had hidden under her blanket. As it slipped from the bed, Rosa grabbed the book before it hit the floor. Señora Martinez had ridiculed her many times for reading the Bible. Rosa didn't want to see her anymore that night, especially now with a Bible in her lap.

Slowly Rosa turned the pages, sometimes reading verses she had learned in school that made her feel better. She stopped at a verse that was marked and read it to herself. *Christ died for our sins, He was buried and rose again.* Her eyes wandered across the room to a picture of Christ on the cross. *I wonder why some people hang pictures showing Jesus being dead. The Bible says He is alive.* A sob caught in her throat. *Oh, María, I wish you were alive. I wish I could see you and Mama and Papa. I'm . . . I'm so lonely.*

Show Illustration #11

Suddenly she remembered a Bible class from the Children's Home. As if it had happened the day before, she recalled something Mrs. Peters had said: "He will be a friend who is always with you." What else had the missionary said? Rosa stared at the verse in her Bible. *Mrs. Peters asked if we believed Jesus died and rose again and was punished for our sin,* Rosa thought. *And, she said to talk to her after class if we did.*

Rosa sighed. *I . . . I wish I could believe in Jesus, but I'm afraid. I do wish I had Him for a friend. Mrs. Peters said He loves me.* She turned off the light and cried herself to sleep.

Rosa continued to work for Señora Martinez for another year and a half. Finally, when Rosa was fourteen, Señora Martinez sent her back to the village. Her little sister was ill and her mother needed help.

One day while Mama washed clothes at the creek, Rosa cleaned the hut and took care of Felicia. Sharp cries sounded across the room. "Oh, ohhh. Ohhh, ohhh." Rosa hurried to where Felicia lay curled on a petate. She was asleep. "Oh, ohhh. Ohhh, ohhh." The crying quavered again outside the hut. Rosa tiptoed to the doorway, but no one was around. "Oh, ohhh. Ohhh, ohhh." The eerie noises continued. Rosa's heart beat rapidly. "It's the spirits," she whispered. "Oh, I wish Mama were here. I hope she comes soon."

Show Illustration #16

As Rosa crossed the room, she noticed her Bible on a shelf. *Maybe if I read that I will not be afraid,* she thought. She sat on a bench, opened the book and began reading aloud. The crying ceased. But when she paused to check Felicia, the crying started again. Quickly Rosa picked up her Bible and read aloud. The crying stopped! Outside the hut, a twig snapped. Rosa stiffened with fear.

"What are you doing, Rosa?" Grandmother demanded as she entered the hut.

"I . . . I heard strange, crying noises," Rosa said weakly. She looked up at Grandmother and trembled. "As long as I read the Bible, I didn't hear them. But when I stopped. . ."

"The crying continued," Grandmother finished for her. She hobbled over to where Felicia stirred on her mat. "Rosa, you heard the spirit of the Weeping Woman. Her crying means your sister will die."

"No!" Rosa shouted, kneeling beside her sister as if to protect her. "No, she cannot die. We are taking care of her. And Mama and Papa are praying for her." She gently caressed Felicia's hair.

Grandmother said nothing. When Rosa looked up again, the doorway was empty. That night Mama and Papa listened as Rosa recounted Grandmother's warning. "Rosa," Papa said in a tired voice, "we have prayed for Felicia. If God wants to heal her, He will. If not, He will take her to heaven to be with Him. I know Grandmother believes in the Weeping Woman, but God is more powerful than evil spirits. If Felicia dies, we will know God answered our prayers in a better way." He paused, then continued. "Yes, a better way even though for a while it will hurt us knowing Felicia is not with us."

Felicia did die, and Rosa became even more afraid of Grandmother. Now with both sisters dead, she felt lonelier than ever. She worked hard and tried to ignore the lonely, empty feeling she had inside.

One hot afternoon as Rosa approached her home, she heard a familiar voice. Quietly she entered and stood inside the doorway. Mrs. Peters was having coffee and bread with Mama.

"Rosa," Mama said, "look who's here! Mrs. Peters has come and we have had a good visit. She wants to take some oranges back to the Children's Home. Please gather them for her."

Show Illustration #17

"May I go with you, Rosa?" asked the missionary. "Your mother and I have finished our coffee. It's been so long since I've seen you." Rosa nodded. Together they walked out to the orange trees.

Standing under a tree, Rosa lifted a long, forked branch behind an orange high overhead. With a twist of the pole the fruit dropped to the ground. As Mrs. Peters put the orange in a basket, she asked, "How have you been, Rosa? You've grown so tall."

"I've been fine most of the time."

"Did you ever find a best friend?" Mrs. Peters asked.

Rosa looked startled. "No . . . no, I never did. But how did you know I wanted one?"

Mrs. Peters laughed. "You always looked at the other children so wistfully at school. You never seemed to have anyone with whom to share your good times."

"No, I didn't," Rosa replied. "I still would like to have a best friend."

"You can, Rosa," Mrs. Peters said gently. "There is someone who wants to be your friend. It's Jesus."

"Yes," interrupted Rosa, "I know. But I'm afraid to believe in Him. Grandmother taught me about the spirit world. She threatened to do something to me if I believe. I remember how the spirits control and hurt people."

"Rosa, Satan has put this fear in your heart because he doesn't want you to accept the Lord Jesus as your Savior," explained the missionary.

"Sometimes I want to believe," Rosa admitted, "but there is a struggle inside me. Part of me says, 'yes, believe,' and part of me says, 'no.'"

Mrs. Peters looked at her kindly. "Rosa," she said, "there will always be a struggle until you ask Jesus to forgive your sin and make you His. Only then will He give you peace."

"I do want my fears to go away, and. . .and my sin forgiven," Rosa said longingly.

"All you need to do, Rosa, is tell God that you have sinned. Ask Him to forgive you." The missionary hesitated, then added, "Would you like to pray now?"

Rosa nodded. "I do believe Jesus died for my sin." She bowed her head and prayed simply, asking God to forgive her sin and make her His child. Looking up, she smiled. "I know He has forgiven me."

Mrs. Peters hugged her. "The Bible says, 'I will never leave you nor forsake you.' That means Jesus will be with you all the time."

"A Friend who will be with me forever," Rosa exclaimed happily.

Chapter 4
TRAINING TO SERVE HER FRIEND

The *aim* of the lesson:

1. To emphasize that God wants Christians to study the Bible so they can tell others how to be saved
2. To show how Bible schools on the mission field prepare Christians to serve among their own people

The verse to be memorized:

Continue . . . in the things which thou hast learned. . . . That from a child thou hast known the holy scriptures which are able to make thee wise unto salvation through faith . . . in Christ Jesus. (2 Timothy 3:14a-15)

The embers snapped on the mud stove. Rosa pulled sticks from the wood pile and laid them on the flickering coals. The fire must be hot for the tortillas.

She crossed the room to the table and began grinding corn on the stone slab. Squeak-pause-squeak. The table swayed with her movements. Quickly she patted the cornmeal into flat cakes and slapped them on the baking dish. Since Felicia's death three years ago, Rosa had assumed more duties for Mama. She looked out through the doorway. *Mama and Papa should be here soon,* she thought, placing the last tortilla on the plate.

Dinner was noisy that night. It always was when Mama and Papa returned from market. The questions her brothers asked! They were outside now, eating the candy her parents brought them. Rosa cleared the table as Mama began washing dishes. Papa stood in the doorway watching the sky darken. He turned as they finished straightening the cooking area.

Show Illustration #19

"Rosa," he said seriously, "I want to ask you an important question. You don't have to answer tonight." He hesitated, "Would you like to go to Bible school?"

Rosa stared at her father. "Bible school?" she asked unbelievingly.

"Yes," Papa replied. "Mama and I saw Mr. and Mrs. Peters at market today. They mentioned that Bible school starts in a few weeks. You are old enough to attend."

Rosa's mind whirled. The Bible school was located beside the Children's Home in town. She remembered eating in the dining hall with the older students.

"How long would I be there?" she asked.

"Five years," Papa answered. "Four years are spent studying in the classroom."

"And the fifth year?" Rosa looked puzzled.

"During the fifth year a student practices what he's learned. He goes out to the villages to teach and help in the churches," Papa said. "If the student does well, at the next graduation he receives his diploma. Rosa, we want you to pray about this before you decide. You work well with children. Our Indian churches need teachers to help the children learn about God."

That night Rosa lay awake for a long time thinking about Papa's question. *Should I go to Bible school?* she wondered. *Five years is a long time. I haven't been in a class or studied for seven years, not since I was ten.* She rolled over on her petate and thought about the classes, homework, and tests. *I would like to study the Bible. But it would be so hard since I never finished school.*

Suddenly a Bible verse flashed into her thoughts. God seemed to whisper to her *"I will never leave you nor forsake you." Thank you, God, for reminding me that You will help me,* she prayed silently. *I don't have to be afraid because You will be with me.*

Show Illustration #20

School *was* hard. Rosa wasn't surprised by all she had to do. *I don't know if I can make it through all this studying,* she worried. There were books to read, papers to write, tests to take. She listened carefully as teachers taught the Bible. Sometimes they demonstrated ways to teach children. Other times they told how to explain the Gospel. There was much to learn.

On weekends, Rosa went with an older student to an outlying village. Other students, in teams of two or three, went to different villages where they practiced what they learned.

"Will we always go to the same place, Lupita?" Rosa asked as they hiked along a narrow mountain trail.

"Oh, no!" replied Lupita. "We take turns going to all the villages. Sometimes we travel by bus. There's a tiny village up here in the mountains. The only way to reach it is by crossing a wobbly rope bridge over a river. But we're not going there today."

"What will we do this weekend?" Rosa inquired.

"There's a small church in the village where we're going," Lupita said. "Sunday morning we'll sing some songs and probably be asked to tell how we accepted the Lord Jesus as our Savior. In the afternoon, you and I will visit people in their homes. Usually people listen as I explain how to be saved, but sometimes they won't. We'll stay with one of the Christian families in the village."

At the beginning of Rosa's third year, a teacher met with the third and fourth-year students. "This year you will be group leaders on weekend ministries. Do you remember how difficult it was to give a testimony or teach a lesson in your first year? We expect you to show the first and second-year students how to teach and witness in the villages."

Later that day, Chela, a first-year student, said to Rosa after classes, "I'm glad I'm going with you this weekend."

Rosa smiled at her. "I've never been the leader before," she admitted. "I'm nervous about our first assignment, but I know God will help us."

Show Illustration #21

The girls left early Saturday morning for a small village. "Do you have everything you need, Chela?" Rosa asked as they headed for the bus stop.

Chela lifted her woven plastic bag. "Bible, hymnbook, clothes, soap," she rattled off. "And an orange–in case I get thirsty from walking."

"I have the Bible lessons and some tracts," Rosa replied as they boarded the crowded bus. They rode for half an hour. Stepping off, Rosa pointed up the road. "See the opening in the trees? That's the start of the path up to the village. Let's hurry before it gets too hot and dusty on the trail this afternoon."

When they arrived, they stopped at the first home on the edge of the village. A dog trotted from behind the hut and barked. "These people are believers, Chela. We'll probably stay here tonight." Rosa looked around and thought, *This reminds me of home.* Streaks of sunlight fell through the trees and cast splashes of light on the dusty ground. A hen scratched in the dirt, then clucked to her chicks as the girls approached.

A short, plump woman came out of the house. "Come," she called, smiling and motioned them inside. "I have bread and coffee ready." The woman's children danced around excitedly. One girl crept close to Rosa and whispered, "Will you have a Sunday school class for us?"

"Yes," Rosa told her happily. The children shouted and ran off. "They've gone to tell their friends, Chela. We must pray that parents will let their children come tomorrow."

Show Illustration #22

Throughout Saturday, the girls visited many of the families and invited children to Sunday school. Sometimes Rosa led a Bible study in an Indian home. On Sunday morning when the children were dismissed from the service, they ran eagerly outdoors. Rosa patiently gathered them under a tree. Chela sat among the children to watch Rosa and learn how to teach.

Rosa's heart beat rapidly as she looked into their eager faces. "Help me, God, to teach these children about You. Help them understand this lesson," she prayed silently.

"Children, look around and tell me what you see," Rosa said.

"Plants. Orange trees. A birdie. My dog. Clouds," called boys and girls.

"You are all right," Rosa said and smiled. "The Bible tells us God made all things." Then she told them the story of creation. God, who created the heavens and the earth, loved them. He sent His perfect Son, the Lord Jesus Christ, to die for their sin. "He wants you to live with Him in heaven someday," Rosa said. She explained how God could forgive them and give them everlasting life.

On Monday morning, the girls walked back to the main road. "Chela," Rosa said as they waited for the bus, "I was fearful when we left Saturday morning. I wasn't sure I could teach without an older student along to help me. As I began the lesson, I realized God was helping me."

Show Illustration #20

Classes continued and there were many more weekend trips. Some days Rosa doubted if she would ever finish school. There was so much to learn. One afternoon near the end of her fourth year, Rosa struggled to write a paper for class.

"Rosa! Rosa, come here!" Chela called urgently as she ran into the dormitory. "Your father is outside . . . with your mother . . . She's ill."

Rosa ran to the door. Papa and some men were walking slowly up the hill carrying Mama on a chair. "What's wrong, Papa?" she cried running to them. She looked at Mama who was strapped to the chair. Her eyes were closed.

"She has a fever, Rosa. She was too weak to walk from the village. Antonio, Pedro, and I took turns carrying her. The doctor must see her." The men carried her into the building.

Show Illustration #23

Rosa didn't take her eyes off the doctor as he examined her mother. She held her breath when he turned to them.

"Your wife has typhoid fever," he said to Papa. "She must stay here where she can be cared for. Rosa, you and one of the missionaries will be the only ones allowed in this room. It will be several weeks before your mother is strong enough to return to the village. Can you watch your mother and keep up with your school work, too?"

"I . . . I must care for Mama," Rosa cried. "I . . . I will study as much as I can."

Rosa rose early every morning and studied late in the evening. It was hard to care for Mama, go to classes and prepare assignments. "Dear God," she prayed daily, "please help mother get well. And . . . and please help me concentrate on my studies so I can finish this year."

One morning Mama called weakly from her bed, "Rosa, you are good to help me while I am sick. I think I feel a little stronger today." She sat up slowly. "Have I kept you from studying?"

"No, Mama," Rosa answered. "God has helped me. I will finish this year with those in my class."

The students prepared special activities for graduation. Now that Mama was getting better and stronger every day, Rosa could help with the plans.

Finally graduation week arrived. Mama, though weak, attended with Papa and the other visitors. The students acted out a Bible story one evening. Then came the banquet and graduation.

I'm glad Mama is well and can enjoy graduation, Rosa thought as she looked across the crowd at her parents.

Just then the graduation speaker stood. "Some of you think this ceremony means the end of your studies," Pastor Felix began. "But you have only begun. During the next year, all fourth-year students will be assigned to work in villages. You will help in our churches, you will teach our Sunday school classes, and you will tell others about the Lord Jesus. If you do well and are faithful in your work, you will receive your diploma at next year's graduation."

Rosa watched as students, who had completed their five years of training, received diplomas. *I wonder if I'll get mine next year. Please Lord, help me to be faithful to You as I teach Your Word in the village where I am assigned.*

Chapter 5
SERVICE FOR HER FRIEND

The *aim* of the lesson:

1. To emphasize that God has chosen believers to serve Him
2. To illustrate how some national believers in Latin America serve the Lord

The verse to be memorized:

Ye have not chosen me, but I have chosen you, and ordained you, that ye should go and bring forth fruit, and that your fruit should remain. (John 15:16a)

Show Illustration #25

Rosa glanced at the diploma in her hand. *Last year I wondered if I'd earn this. How good God has been to help me.* She smiled as she looked around the graduation crowd. Shouts and laughter surrounded her.

"Rosa! Rosa!" a voice called impatiently beside her. "Show me your diploma again," one of her brothers pleaded.

"Later, at home," she answered. "Look over there," Rosa said and nodded her head towards the road.

Two young boys ran around the little groups of people. *Their hair is the color of corn,* she thought. She watched a slender woman grab one of the boys as he dashed by. *She must be their mother.*

"Who are they?" her brother asked. He stared at the boy who tugged on his mother's arm.

"They must be the new missionaries," Rosa said. "See, there is their father." A tall man with dark glasses swung the younger boy onto his shoulders. Just then the mother glanced over at them and smiled. Rosa smiled at her before following her brothers. They had raced down the hill to the street where their parents waited.

It was late afternoon when the family reached their village. Rosa spread her diploma on the table. Her brothers elbowed each other as they leaned over the diploma to look at the paper.

"When I was working in the village on the other side of the mountain, I wasn't sure I would get my diploma," Rosa said to her parents. "It was difficult work. Some people there believe in false spirits as Grandmother did." Remembering Grandmother, Rosa added, "I was happy when you sent a message saying she accepted the Lord Jesus before she died. God was good to answer our prayers for her."

Rosa paused to look outside as several children ran past shouting to each other. She turned to her parents and said, "Sometimes the children in that village wouldn't sit still and listen to the Bible lessons. But other times people wanted to know more about God. I knew God was with me because He showed me how to teach them."

She reached for her diploma, crossed the room and laid it carefully on a shelf. "God is good. I could not have received this diploma without His help." She turned to help Mama prepare supper.

Several weeks later Rosa walked into town to market by herself because Mama was ill again. When she stopped at the Bible school before heading back to the village, Mrs. Peters greeted her.

"Rosa, do you have time to meet our new missionaries?" she asked.

"Yes, it's still early. I would like to meet them," Rosa replied. She and Mrs. Peters walked towards one of the homes on the property.

A laughing, blond-haired boy burst out of the doorway, followed by an older boy at his heels. They stopped when they saw Rosa.

"This is Stephen. He's the oldest," Mrs. Peters explained. "And this is Jon."

The boys grinned and ran around the house.

"They don't speak Spanish very well," Mrs. Peters said.

The slender, dark-haired woman Rosa had seen at graduation came to the door. "Rosa, this is Hermana Joy. Hermano Thomas is not here now. He is visiting in one of the villages with my husband." (Believers in Mexico call each other sister and brother because they belong to the family of God.)

Show Illustration #26

Rosa smiled at the missionary. *Joy is a good name for her,* Rosa thought. *She looks happy.*

Joy smiled at the young Indian woman. "Rosa, I need someone to help me in our home," she said hesitantly in Spanish. "And we need someone to translate into Aztec when we go into villages. Mrs. Peters says you are a good worker, and that you know both languages. Would you be able to help us?"

Rosa was startled. "I . . . I don't know," she stammered, "but I'll pray about it." Later on the trail, Rosa's thoughts were jumbled. *What shall I do? I would like to help Hermana Joy. She seems nice. But Mama is just beginning to recover. I should stay to help her. . . . But then, town isn't too far away, and I would like to help in the village churches. I could do that if I translated for the missionaries.* Rosa stopped suddenly outside her village. *Oh, they probably won't eat our kind of food. Dear God, I don't know what to do. Show me where You want me to serve You.*

That night as Rosa poured coffee for her parents, she said, "Maybe I could help them just for a few months." She handed Mama a cup. "It would be different living with them. But if it didn't work out, I could come home."

"Yes, you could come back, Rosa, and we would be glad to have you," Papa replied. "But you've studied for five years, and now I believe it's time for you to help our people understand the Bible."

When Mama was well again, Rosa moved into town with the missionary family. *They speak so much English,* Rosa thought as she cleaned the house. Each week she understood a few more words, but she was too shy to pronounce them. The sounds were too strange.

"Rosa," called Joy one Saturday morning several months later. "I would like to take a group of Bible school girls to one of the villages. Will you show us the way?"

"Oh, yes, Hermana Joy," Rosa said eagerly.

The small group headed for a nearby village in the mountains. "This trail," Rosa explained, pointing to a path, "leads to a family who does not believe. The next trail takes us where you want to go." Rosa led the women up the trail and into a clearing. A young girl was playing with a baby in front of a thatched hut. Her mother was grinding corn on a table nearby. She looked up and greeted them in Aztec.

Show Illustration #27

Rosa turned to Joy and translated into Spanish, "She welcomes you and wants you to stay for a meal." Looking at the girls, Rosa said, "All of us should help prepare the food. Someone bring water from the creek for cooking. Maybe one of you will grind more corn for our hostess?"

Joy watched the woman take the cornmeal and pat it flat. "She makes it look so easy," Joy remarked to Rosa.

"Would you like to make a tortilla?" Rosa asked the missionary. She handed Joy some meal.

Joy patted and stretched the corn dough. The girls laughed when she held up a square tortilla full of holes. The woman chuckled, took the misshapen dough, and remade it.

Back in town that evening, Rosa confided to Joy, "I enjoy helping you. It was good to pray and talk with the girls after our Bible study with the woman and her daughter."

Joy smiled as she said, "I'm glad you are happy working with us, Rosa. You understood the girls' problems today and knew what Bible verses would help them." She paused. "Rosa, I'll need your help even more in a few months when our baby is born. I won't be able to teach Stephen and Jon and care for the baby at the same time."

Show Illustration #28

"And I need your help before my wife does," said Hermano Thomas entering the room. He sat on the couch beside Joy and rubbed his mustache. "I'm taking some of the students back to the village we visited last week. Will you come with us, Rosa, and act as translator? I could conduct the Bible study in Spanish, but the Indians will understand it better in Aztec."

"I would like to help," Rosa replied eagerly.

The next afternoon the van bounced over the rough road. *It's been a long trip,* Rosa thought hours later as they drove into the village. She leaned out of the open window and waved at a child playing in the dirt.

"The sons of the devil are back," a shrill voice called out from one of the buildings. The child leaped to his feet and ran into the nearest house. Other children up the street scurried into their homes.

Rosa ducked back into the van and glanced at Hermano Thomas. "Someone has spread rumors about you. Many of these people believe in the spirits and some are Catholics. It won't be easy to talk to them. (*Teacher:* Delete "some are Catholics" if this would be objectionable to some students.)

Thomas steered the van to the side of the road and stopped before a small house. "Juan and his family live here. Last week when we were here he agreed to let us have a Bible study in his home."

Everyone scrambled out of the van. Juan stepped from the house. His dark eyes darted around the village. "Come, come," he said motioning quickly.

Show Illustration #29

Inside, Juan pulled chairs to the table. Thomas opened his Bible and read. Then Rosa translated as he explained the verses. After a while Juan's wife lit a kerosene lamp and placed it on the table. Rosa moved to the window and peered out. In the darkness she saw a flash of light and then another and another. The lights grew brighter as they came closer to the house. She watched a group of men carrying lanterns circle the house. A glint of shiny metal caught her eye. She gasped and bit her lip. A machete!

Thump! Crash! Rocks clattered against the roof. Voices screamed, "Evangelicals come to divide us! We live together in peace! We do not need another religion! We do not want you here. Get out of our village."

Juan jumped up and moved to the window. Thomas stood and put his hand on the Indian's shoulder. "Juan, we will pray. God will take care of you and us." He bowed his head, "Dear Lord, we know You brought us here to tell Juan and his family about Jesus. Protect them. Please calm the angry men outside and allow us to leave safely. Make it possible for us to return to teach these people more about You."

Thomas started to sing and motioned the students to join. Softly, then louder and more confidently they sang. When they finished, a gruff voice outdoors called, "Juan, let us in to talk with that missionary."

Several men entered and stood in front of the door. A few grasped their machete handles. "Why have you come?" demanded an older man striding over to Thomas.

"We have come to teach you what the Bible says about the Lord Jesus," Rosa translated for him.

"Well, we don't like what you teach," another man growled. He looked at the group of students. "How could you sing? Didn't you know we had machetes?" He fingered the one by his side. "Why aren't you afraid now?"

One of the students spoke bravely, "God has taken away our fear."

"Humph!" A short man stepped forward. "We do not want you to come back," he threatened shaking his fist.

"If you do return," said the old man looking at Rosa and the students, "we might harm that van or run you out of town."

After more threats and loud swearing, the men left. Rosa watched the lanterns flicker in the distance until all was darkness. After comforting Juan and his family, Thomas led the group out to the van. Rosa settled back on a seat. She closed her eyes as the vehicle bounced over the rutted roads.

Dear Jesus, she prayed silently, *thank you for protecting us. Show us when we should return to tell these people more about You. Without You, they will be in darkness as black as the night around us. They need to know that You are the Light of the world. They need You as their Friend.*

Show Illustration #28

It was late when the van pulled into the Bible school. Joy listened without saying a word as Rosa and Thomas described their escape.

"Hermana Joy, Hermano Thomas," Rosa said, "before I knew Jesus, I was like those people in that village. I was afraid of the spirits. I was afraid to believe in Jesus. But one day, many years after I heard the Gospel, I chose to believe in Jesus as my Savior. He was the One I longed for as a friend. God directed me to Bible school where I learned how to serve Him. There must be some people in that village who will believe some day. Maybe God has chosen me to go back there and tell them the Gospel."

"Maybe you are to go back, Rosa," Joy said softly. "Let's pray for others to join us so we can reach the people in that village and other villages with the Gospel."

Teacher: Conclude with a missionary challenge. Adapt the following questions to specific missionaries or projects which your students know.

Show Front Cover

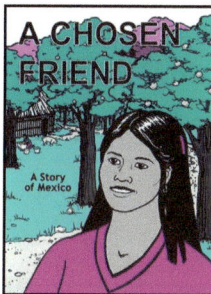

Will you go someday and help missionaries like Joy, Thomas and Rosa teach others about God?

Will you pray faithfully–every day– for missionaries you know?

Will you give some of your money to missions?

www.ingramcontent.com/pod-product-compliance
Lightning Source LLC
Chambersburg PA
CBHW042019080426
42735CB00002B/103